DAVID STONE

EIGHT PIECES
IN THE THIRD POSITION
FOR VIOLIN AND PIANO

Extra Violin parts available

NOVELLO PUBLISHING LIMITED
8/9 Frith Street, London W1V 5TZ

Order No: NOV 120051

EIGHT PIECES
for Third Position of the Violin
with Piano accompaniment

First and Second Fingers only

DAVID STONE

1. MARCH in D

4

Without the Fourth Finger

2. MARCH in G

18416

Without the Fourth Finger

3. NOCTURNE

18416

Without the Fourth Finger

4. COUNTRY DANCE

18416

8

Without the Fourth Finger

5. BERCEUSE

18416

Including the Fourth Finger

6. FESTIVE DANCE

18416

Introducing harmonics

7. PASTORALE

8. INTERMEZZO

20

7/96 (24632)